AF228877

EXPLORING EGYPTIAN MYTHOLOGY

Don Nardo

San Diego, CA

© 2024 ReferencePoint Press, Inc.
Printed in the United States

For more information, contact:
ReferencePoint Press, Inc.
PO Box 27779
San Diego, CA 92198
www.ReferencePointPress.com

LIBRARY OF CONGRESS CATALOGING-IN-PUBLICATION DATA

Names: Nardo, Don, 1947- author.
Title: Exploring Egyptian mythology / Don Nardo.
Description: San Diego : ReferencePoint Press, 2023. | Includes
   bibliographical references and index.
Identifiers: LCCN 2023023108 (print) | LCCN 2023023109 (ebook) | ISBN
   9781678207281 (library binding) | ISBN 9781678207298 (ebook)
Subjects: LCSH: Mythology, Egyptian. | Gods, Egyptian. | Egypt--Religion.
Classification: LCC BL2441.3 .N3645 2023 (print) | LCC BL2441.3 (ebook)
   | DDC 299/.3113--dc23/eng20230911
LC record available at https://lccn.loc.gov/2023023108
LC ebook record available at https://lccn.loc.gov/2023023109

CONTENTS

Blueprints for Life

As recalled in one of ancient Egypt's chief myths, shortly after the earth was divinely created—far back in the mists of time—the dual-gendered fertility god Hapi appeared. Guided by Khnum, a ram-headed creator god, Hapi took up residence in a cave located near Elephantine. This small island in the Nile River marked Egypt's southernmost border at the time and was perceived as the source of the great river. A set of huge, sturdy doors blocked the entrance to the cave on Elephantine, and just outside that barrier dwelled a guardian serpent that was so big and fierce that even the river's crocodiles were afraid to swim nearby.

Although powerful in many ways, Hapi lacked the ability to unlock and open the cave doors. The only being who had that power was Khnum, who presided over Egypt's all-important river. Khnum assigned Hapi the job of controlling the Nile floodwaters each year. The river itself, Khnum initially explained to Hapi, had two sources. One lay far to the south of Egypt. The other source was in the distant and mysterious land of the dead; from there that unseen branch of the great waterway meandered through the heavens until it reached Hapi's cave, where for most of each year the great doors held back the torrents that would, when released, flood the river's banks in Egypt.

Every July, Khnum unlocked those doors. Then it was Hapi's task to guide the sacred waters built up behind them as they merged with the waters from the terrestrial source in the distant south and steadily made their way downstream, past Elephantine, and into the rest of Egypt. Fortunately for the residents of that ancient land, the deluge, which they called the inundation, was slow moving and gentle and ensured the fertility of the crops planted along the river. Indeed, "the Nile performed an annual miracle," says Egyptologist Toby Wilkinson. The river sent

> a torrent of water downstream (in this case north). By early August the approaching inundation was clearly discernible [and] a few days later, the flood arrived in earnest. With an unstoppable force, the Nile burst its banks, and the waters spread out over the floodplain . . . along the entire length of the Nile Valley. For several weeks, all the cultivable land was underwater. . . . [The] inundation brought with it the potential for new life, [for] once the flood retreated, the soil emerged again, fertilized and irrigated, ready for the sowing of crops. It was thanks to this annual phenomenon that Egypt enjoyed such productive agriculture.[1]

Hymn to Hapi

Quite appropriately, the Egyptians also called the inundation "Hapi's arrival," for they believed that the god's life force literally pushed the floodwaters forward. Therefore, by standing in the spreading waters or riding a boat over them, the people of the Nile Valley enjoyed brief moments of direct contact with that divine being. Happily, each summer they held celebrations to thank Hapi for the gifts of irrigation, fertility, and plentiful harvests. That these boons made Egyptian civilization possible is what inspired the fifth-century-BCE Greek historian Herodotus to remark that "Egypt, to which we sail nowadays, is, as it were, the gift of the river."[2]

Herodotus did not know how long such celebrations had been taking place because he had no idea how old Egyptian civilization was. Modern historians now know that thriving farming communities had evolved along the Nile's banks at least as early as 4000 BCE, over thirty-five centuries before that Greek scholar's time. And some evidence shows that the worship of gods associated with the river was already well-established even then.

At the annual summer festivals dedicated to those gods, people all over the country sang hymns to Hapi. Excerpts from one of them stated, "Hail to thee, O Nile! You show yourself in this land, coming in peace, giving life to Egypt. . . . Shine forth in glory, O Nile!"[3] The celebrants also danced, feasted, and worshipped Hapi and Khnum at various shrines. From time to time during these festivities, Egyptian priests called on skilled artists from far and wide to create wall paintings of Hapi (some of which survive today). Those artists pictured him with green skin, to symbolize the lush greenery that grew along the river's banks. Painters also depicted Hapi as dual-gendered. On the one hand he was hailed as a father figure and had a male beard; on the other he had heavy, drooping breasts and a protruding pregnant belly, both female traits. The reason for these depictions of combined genders was to suggest that Hapi was both the father and mother of the Nile and thereby a fruitful producer of new life and one who ensured the continuance of life in the region.

It is important to point out that the paintings, hymn singing, dancing, and other forms of worship associated with the god of the inundation were deeply and earnestly felt by the Egyptian people. True, the artistic depictions of Hapi as a sort of unisex deity were intended mainly to be symbolic. However, the worshippers seriously and completely believed that Hapi was real; similarly, they held that the events of the myth about Hapi and Khnum had occurred in a past age. In the same way, the tales of the many other Egyptian deities were accepted as actual historical events. The general belief was that such stories were key incidents that had long ago brought about the creation of the earth, animals, humans, and the social customs of everyday life.

Such steadfast belief in the authenticity of a collection of myths could have occurred *only* with people who were extremely religiously devout. And that was in fact the case with the ancient Egyptians. In the book Herodotus penned following his months-long visit to Egypt, he famously remarked that its inhabitants "are religious to excess, beyond any other nation in the world."[4] As a result of that high degree of religious devotion, the Egyptians viewed their ancient tales of the gods the same way people today see the histories of their nations and the world. Egypt's myths also provided people guidance in how to worship the gods, how to obey the nation's leaders, and how to live righteous lives. Thus, the age-old myths were in a very real sense blueprints for life.

CHAPTER ONE

Maintaining the Natural Order

Word swiftly spread through the ranks of the Egyptian gods and goddesses that one of their number—Hathor—had flown into a rage. Wisely, they all shied away because they knew what horrors that daughter of the sun god, Ra, could unleash when she was angry. They were also aware of the strange duality of her personality. Most of the time, she adopted the head of a peaceful cow and acted as a pleasant motherly figure who cared deeply for her children. She was also widely known and loved for being a deity of joy who had an expansive sense of humor. Now and then, however, Hathor's fellow divinities knew, all those kindly, caring qualities momentarily fell away. When sufficiently provoked, she exploded into a sort of mindless fury. Donning the head of a lioness, in that state she was capable of acts of extreme violence and cruelty.

This time was no exception. What had provoked Hathor's current wrath was finding out that her divine father, Ra—Egypt's king in the land's mythic past—had been disrespected by a group of mere humans. That group's leaders claimed that Ra was a poor ruler who did not deserve to oversee Egypt. Furthermore, the legend claims they plotted to replace him on the throne with a human king. The sun god decided that these insolent rebels must be punished and began asking other deities for suggestions for what form the penalty should take.

Hearing of these events, Hathor, who took pride in being one of her father's most faithful protectors, could not contain her anger. In her fevered mind she felt there was only one way to deal with the impudent humans; they must be eradicated from existence. Not waiting for orders from her father, she leaped upward, flew across Egypt, and quickly found the conspirators. Grabbing them two and three at a time, she used her lioness's claws to tear them limb from limb and then drank their blood.

Not long afterward, Ra heard what his daughter was up to and hurried to the scene of the slaughter. There, to his regret, he saw that after slaying the rebels she was not yet satisfied and was now attacking innocent people as well. Worried that Hathor might wipe out the entire human race, the divine ruler resorted to trickery. He had some helpers bring him large quantities of beer that had been stained red to look like blood. When Hathor saw what she assumed was lots of human blood, she rapidly slurped it up. And just as her father had hoped, she soon fell into a drunken stupor. In the hours that followed, she forgot about punishing humanity and took a long nap.

Turning to Gods and Myths Rather than History

When the other gods and goddesses heard that Hathor's rampage was over, they were relieved. In the weeks that followed, as a playful jest, they nicknamed her the Lady of Drunkenness. She did not take offense, for her famous sense of humor had come back. As Hathor's peaceful nature returned, Ra went back to ruling Egypt and riding his blindingly bright solar barge across the sky each day. Likewise, Osiris went back to his job as ruler of the underworld, the jackal-headed Anubis once more protected tombs and cemeteries, Thoth resumed his duties as divine scribe, and Hapi continued to prepare for bringing the next Nile River flood.

These six deities were only a tiny handful of those in Egypt's great religious pantheon, or total collection of gods and goddesses. Today no one knows for sure how many there were in all. This is because long before Egypt became the world's first

Ra, the sun god of the Egyptians, is depicted riding his sun barge across the sky.

nation-state in about 3100 BCE, that land consisted of hundreds of small towns spread out over a large expanse of territory. Each town or region had its own local patron deities. And as the centuries wore on, some of those gods gained national importance and were worshipped by all; a few disparate deities merged into one, assuming a new and different image, powers, and duties; and other gods faded into obscurity and were forgotten.

One thing that all these gods had in common over the country's long history was that the Egyptians were certain they were real. Also, each deity oversaw one or more aspects, or niches, of life and nature. Moreover, the general belief was that the gods had created the world and humanity; possessed magical, super-human powers; watched over and judged the actions and worth of people; and had to be regularly worshipped to ensure that nature's order and balance—called *maat*—survived.

In fact, modern scholars think that the Egyptians' belief in the maintenance of the natural order was what guided their conception of this assemblage of divine beings in the first place. First, it was clear to people that their ancestors had lacked the powers to create the huge and complex world. Therefore, superior beings that did possess the necessary powers must exist.

Second, those beings—the gods—desired that the world always remain largely as they had created it. The evidence for this idea seemed obvious to the early Egyptians. Indeed, in their eyes, change within the natural, physical scheme of things was almost undetectable. Each new generation grew up in a world that was largely the same as it had been in prior generations. This perception of sameness and stability was the reason that the Egyptians had little or no sense of history or progress. As the late historian H.W.F. Saggs put it, "With no concept of social progress, they had no incentive to make a conscious record of life in the thousand years before [their own time]."[5]

This is why the Egyptians did not write formal histories to tell future generations what had happened in the past. Instead, they turned to their extensive assortment of myths. These stories recalled how the gods had created the landforms, seas, sky, and other aspects of the universe, along with plants, animals, and humans. That was the only history most Egyptians needed or wanted. The myths also offered guidance on how to worship the gods and live a proper life. To Egypt's residents, therefore, those tales were timely, relevant, and highly meaningful.

Categorizing the Gods and Myths

If, to ordinary Egyptians, there was a drawback to this collection of myths, it was its sheer vastness. Just as there were huge numbers of gods to learn about and keep track of, there were also a great many ancient stories about those deities. Fortunately for Egypt's populace, they could turn to a class of professionals who, among other important duties, were tasked with recording, reciting, and explaining the myths. These chief interpreters of the gods and myths were members of Egypt's large, powerful priesthood. They managed the gods' temples, guarded sacred statues of the deities that stood within those structures, organized religious festivals dedicated to the gods, and passed on the creation stories and other myths from generation to generation.

To make the many diverse gods and their stories easier to remember and understand, a group of early Egyptian rulers and

Egyptian Mythical Influences on Greece

Over time the Greeks and Romans came to worship several originally Egyptian deities and in general were strongly influenced by certain Egyptian myths and religious customs. The fifth-century-BCE Greek historian Herodotus, today often referred to as the Father of History, acknowledged the Greek social debt to the Egyptians. He paid an extended visit to Egypt in the mid-400s BCE and afterward devoted a large section of his famous history book to Egyptian culture. While in Egypt, Herodotus conferred with several local priests, who told him about Egypt's gods and myths. And both he and they agreed that the early Greeks had borrowed both gods and myths from Egypt. In his book, Herodotus wrote that:

> the Egyptians were the first of men who made solemn assemblies and processions and approaches to the [religious] temples, and from them the [Greeks] have learnt them, and my evidence for this is that the Egyptian celebrations of these have been held from a very ancient time, whereas the [Greek versions] were introduced but lately. . . . [In Egypt] there is a very great temple of Isis. . . . Now Isis is in the tongue of the [Greeks] Demeter [goddess of crops, especially grains].

Herodotus, "An Account of Egypt," trans. G.C. Macaulay, Project Gutenberg, January 25, 2013. www.gutenberg.org.

Members of Egypt's priesthood supervised and protected the gods' sacred temples and artifacts like the one shown here.

priests sorted and categorized them in various ways. One such approach was to classify those deities by their functions and duties. For example, because most Egyptians were farmers, it made sense to create a category of gods associated with crops and the soil's fertility. Among the chief divinities in that group was an early version of Osiris, who, it was thought, ensured the fertility of the soil. Several myths depicted him instructing farmers on how to till the soil in the proper manner; there were also stories that depicted him teaching farming families how to grind grains into flour and bake bread. Also in this category were Neper, the god who gave grain the power to grow, and Geb, who oversaw the growth of green plants.

Another group of gods categorized by their functions were those involved with the basic workings of the universe and natural world. A major example was the sun god Ra, who had been one of Egypt's divine rulers before the human kings—or pharaohs—assumed that duty. Joining him in maintaining the universal order of things was the moon god, Khonsu; Ptah, a creator deity and patron of artisans; and Nut, envisioned as the mother and overseer of the planets and other heavenly bodies.

Also in this group was Thoth, who was thought to possess universal wisdom. Several myths associated with this colorful god told how he invented writing, magic, music, medicine, and many religious rituals. No less important was a myth explaining how Thoth acted as the scribe of the underworld. There, he recorded the names of deceased people after other gods decided their fates. Based on his exploits in that position, he earned the nicknames of He Who Balances and the God of the Equilibrium. Additional tales told how Thoth maintained the library of the gods with the aid of his divine wife, Seshat. He was also credited with composing the *Book of Thoth*, which supposedly contained the most hidden and magical secrets of the universe.

Zoomorphs and Divine Protectors

Another way the early Egyptians classified their gods and the myths associated with them was by physical traits. Most Egyptian deities were pictured in paintings and statues as having human form. However, a subdivision of them was depicted either as animals or as beings that combined human parts with animals' heads or other body parts. Modern Egyptologists (historians who specialize in ancient Egypt) call those part-human, part-animal gods zoomorphs. One of the best known zoomorphs was Hathor, the goddess who usually adopted a cow's head but who could replace it with the visage of a lioness when she was angry. Similarly, the creator god Khnum had a ram's head; and Ammit, a demon goddess associated with death and executions, had a crocodile's head, a leopard's midsection, and a hippo's hind legs.

Perhaps the most famous of the Egyptian zoomorphs today is Anubis, the god of the dead. With his jackal's head, in Egypt's earliest times he was seen as Ra's son. In later ages, however, most Egyptians favored the myths that depicted Anubis as the son of Osiris after the latter became ruler of the underworld. In those tales, Anubis protected the souls of dead people, especially royal and noble individuals, as well as oversaw the process of mummification.

Still another important category of gods included the ones who, the Egyptians held, protected humanity from evil and destructive beings and forces. One of those protectors, for instance—the goddess Taweret—stood guard over women during childbirth. There was also a myth that told how the god Bes protected children, as well as several tales about the origins of Horus, who protected humans overall. Similarly, the god Kherty guarded human souls lying in tombs and grave sites.

Anubis, the god of death and the protector of deceased souls (pictured), supervised the mummification process of those with royal and noble titles.

Fond Hopes for the Life Beyond

Looking at these and other similar categories of gods and their tales, the many references to death, the soul, and the underworld illustrate a powerful theme that recurs throughout Egyptian mythology. It is a strong belief in the reality of an afterlife. Indeed, the ancient Egyptians devoted a hefty proportion of their thoughts and actions to preparing to inhabit a mysterious world they believed existed beyond the one into which they were born. Egyptologist Bob Brier points out that "no civilization ever devoted so much of its energies and resources to the quest for immortality as did Egypt's."[6]

Among those efforts by the living to prepare for the afterlife was for a person to do as many good deeds as possible while alive. It was believed that when the gods judged dead souls, those who had failed to do any good deeds would not make it into the afterlife. Also, a person's body had to be preserved in the best way possible. Mummification was the ideal, although it was expensive; but for the poor, placing the corpse in a sturdy coffin would usually suffice. In addition, various objects from life,

The Versatile Khepri

Of the many Egyptian deities, Khepri was one of the more versatile and fascinating, in large part because he had several different functions and duties and fit into multiple categories of gods. One of his functions was to protect the leading sun god, Ra, as the latter journeyed on his shining barge across the sky each day. Some myths claim that Khepri rode with Ra on the journey. It remains unclear whether the Egyptians conceived of the barge itself as the sun or whether the barge carried the sun. Whichever it was, it was thought that the sun's brightness diminished as the day wore on. So, one of Khepri's other jobs was to replenish the sun's brightness in preparation for the next day. In this way, Khepri became known as a god of resurrection, or renewal, and the residents of some regions saw him as another sun god. In addition, Khepri was a zoomorph because he had the body of a human male and the head of a scarab beetle. (A few surviving wall paintings show him as the opposite—a being with the body of a beetle and a human head.)

including clothes and food, needed to be collected and placed beside the body (for use in the life beyond). Finally, there had to be a proper burial.

Not surprisingly, many Egyptian myths dealt with these and other preparations and steps for reaching the realm of the dead. So powerful and compelling were these stories about eternal life that over time they influenced other ancient Mediterranean cultures. The Greeks and Romans, for instance, borrowed both gods and afterlife-related myths from Egypt. In fact, some of Egypt's gods and myths became widely renowned for capturing the Egyptians' fervent "joy in living" and fond hopes for the life beyond, says historian Joshua J. Mark. "The enduring admiration for Egyptian mythology and the culture it informed is a testimony to the power of the life-affirming message inherent in these ancient tales."[7]

CHAPTER TWO

Tales of the Creator Gods

Well before the earth and humans appeared, all that existed was darkness, and in this darkness stretched a vast, formless sea. At some point in prehistory, that dark ocean became aware of itself and emerged as the first divine being, Nun. More time passed— perhaps a few centuries or maybe thousands of centuries; no one can say for sure. And during all that time, watery Nun remained by himself, solitary and silent, thinking but not overtly acting. Like many Egyptian gods, Nun was often depicted as male, though he had female traits as well.

One of Nun's female aspects was revealed when he "gave birth" to Atum, the primordial god of creation. As the tale goes, Nun felt a turbulence within himself. For hours it grew more intense and painful, until suddenly, out of the first god's immense liquid body sprang his progeny. Later, Atum would recall to his fellow deities, "I lifted myself from the watery mass." Except for dark and quiet Nun, "I was alone. But I took courage in my heart. I laid a foundation."[8]

The "foundation" to which Atum referred was the process by which he set the world's creation in motion. The first step in that process occurred when Atum said his own name. So powerful was his voice that it sent ripples coursing through Nun's gigantic body. Then, wasting no time, Atum created the first patch of dry land—the sacred *ben-ben*; and when he stood on it, he started fashioning other gods. Among them were the twins Shu and Tefnut, constructed from Atum's own bodily fluids. Shu and Tefnut were also loath to waste time, so they swiftly produced two more gods, Geb and Nut. In turn, Geb and Nut fashioned four more divinities—Osiris, Isis, Seth, and Nephthys. Together, Atum and the eight gods who had sprung from his bodily fluids formed the sacred band of nine deities the Egyptians would come to call the Ennead.

As soon as the gods of the Ennead were acquainted with one another, they continued the creation process by forming more land, including mountains, plains, valleys, and beaches. Next, they decided to make humans. For that effort, Atum stepped forward and began to cry. He was not sad; it was because his tears contained the magical ingredients needed to make people. "Men and women arose from tears which came forth from my eye,"[9] the wondrous creator later recalled. Finally, Atum fashioned animals and plants, thereby completing the complex process of creation. And when all this miraculous activity had come to pass, Atum stunned gods and people alike by rising into the sky and transforming himself into the awe-inspiring sun god, Atum-Ra.

Different Versions of a Larger Truth

This whimsical tale—today the best known of ancient Egypt's cosmogonies, or creation stories—originated in the Egyptian town of Heliopolis. Situated where Egypt's modern capital, Cairo, now stands, it was a leading religious center in ancient times. Its powerful priesthood championed the Atum-centered version of creation, which came to be known as the Heliopolitan Cosmogony.

By no means, however, did all Egyptians—whether priests or ordinary people—agree that Atum had created the world and humanity. Indeed, ancient Egypt had three other major cosmogonies, along with a few minor ones. And each one had differences with, or even significantly contradicted, the others.

The main reason that the Egyptians maintained so many distinct creation tales rests with the first pharaoh, Narmer, who brought together the region's hundreds of separate towns into a unified nation. He realized that each town or region had its personal patron gods and creation stories. And he appreciated that these local traditions were deeply imbedded. Rather than force everyone to accept a single cosmogony, he wisely allowed the perpetuation of multiple creation stories. That way he was able to better maintain everyone's support, obedience, and loyalty.

In the modern world, the idea of a religion having many, sometimes contradictory origin tales seems unusual. Most people today are more used to faiths that have only a single creation story, such as those of Judaism, Christianity, and Islam. Particularly peculiar by

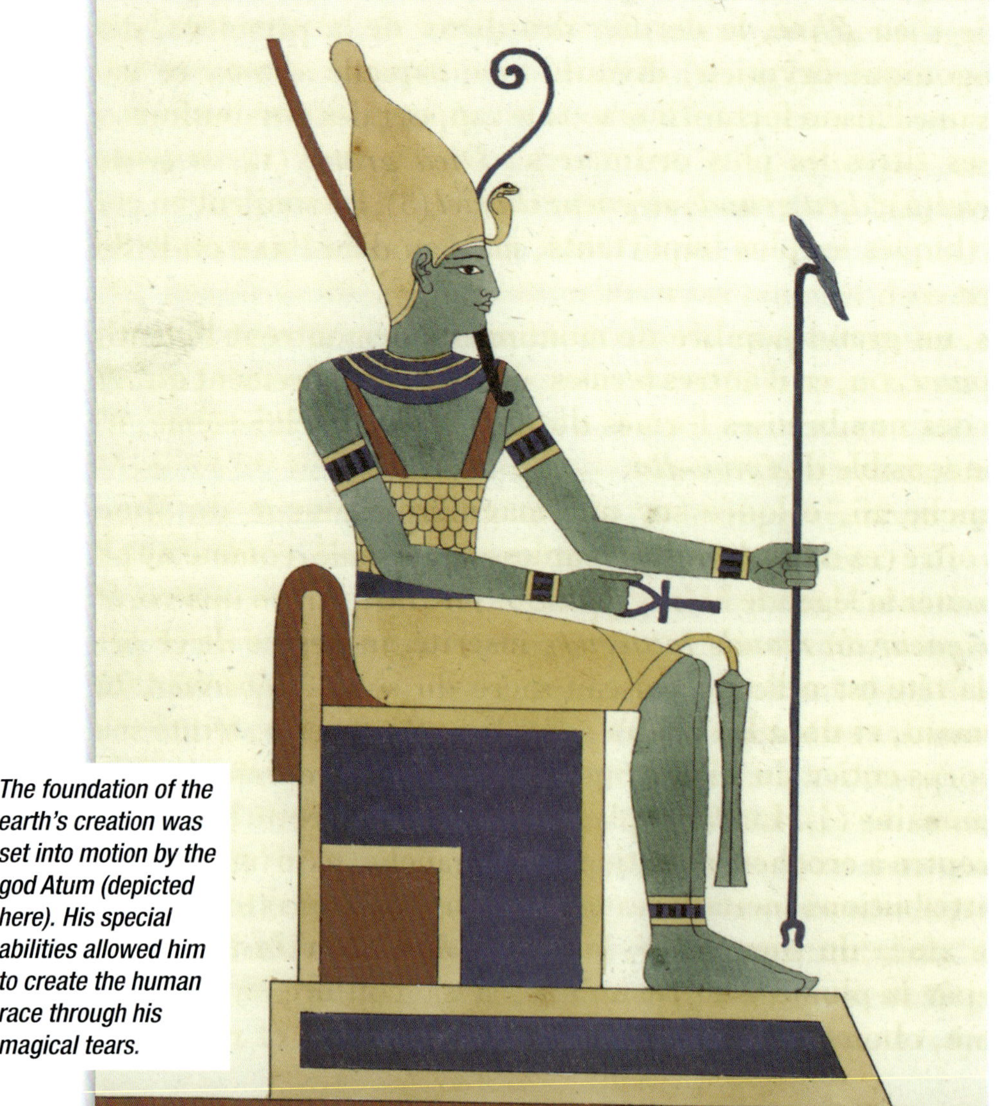

The foundation of the earth's creation was set into motion by the god Atum (depicted here). His special abilities allowed him to create the human race through his magical tears.

modern standards is the fact the Egyptians came to accept all their creation myths as equally valid. But by the Egyptians' own standards, this was not unnerving or problematic because they did not see those divergent tales as literal, factual accounts. Instead, they viewed them more as symbolic in nature and filled with mystery. Moreover, they saw that aura of mystery as compelling and simply accepted that the gods could impart truths and lessons in different ways.

To better explain it, historians sometimes point to a modern parallel—the fact that all modern Christians accept the validity of the four Gospels (Matthew, Mark, Luke, and John) in the Bible's New Testament. Concerned with Jesus's life and preaching, the four accounts contradict one another in various ways, yet Christians tend to look at them as differing versions of a larger underlying and harmonious truth and therefore as equally valid. Similarly, says historian Vincent A. Tobin, the sometimes-conflicting Egyptian cosmogonies still "bore witness to the unity, harmony, and singleness of everything that exists."[10]

Miracle in the Town of the Eight

The degree to which the multiple Egyptian creation myths varied can be seen by comparing the Heliopolitan version to the one favored at Hermopolis, a town located roughly 200 miles (322 km) south of Heliopolis. The Egyptians often referred to Hermopolis as the Town of the Eight. This was a reference to a group of eight deities who played central roles in the myths composing the Hermopolitan Cosmogony. The collective name for those eight gods was the Ogdoad.

A key distinction between the Heliopolitan Ennead and Hermopolitan Ogdoad is how the gods in each group had supposedly come into existence. In the creation tale from Heliopolis, Atum had sprung out of the dark waters of Nun; then he had gone on to

A Controversial Claim About the Sacred Mound

One object that appeared in all of Egypt's creation stories was the first piece of dry land on earth—the sacred ben-ben. In studying surviving ancient Egyptian writings, archaeologists found a controversial claim about the ben-ben made by some priests at Heliopolis. It was that a small section of that holy mound had survived into their era. And, they boasted, it lay inside the temple of Atum at Heliopolis, where members of their order carefully guarded it day and night. There is no way to know for sure whether those priests did watch over an object they thought came from the mound of creation. But if they did, it is certain that most ordinary Egyptians never saw it. This is because of the strict rules and traditions that regulated Egypt's temples. Those structures were not—like modern churches—places where average people gathered to worship. Rather, the inner chambers of Egyptian temples were restricted to priests and kings. Regular citizens—especially poor folk—were excluded. Most Egyptians worshipped the gods either in their homes, in crowds gathered on city streets, or in the countryside during religious festivals.

fashion eight other gods. In contrast, the Hermopolitan creation story claimed that the deities making up the Ogdoad were not physically created by anyone. Instead, in a manner that no one, including the priests, could explain, the members of the Ogdoad had always existed in the waters of the enormous primeval sea.

Initially, those eight sacred beings were shaped like frogs, snakes, and other creatures that dwell in water. Their names were Amun, Amaunet, Hey, Hauhet, Nun, Naunet, Kek, and Kauket. Composed of four male-female pairs, they lived quietly in the dark ocean for many eons, or as some Egyptian priests suggested, perhaps for an infinite time.

One day without warning, however, the eight beings felt an irresistible urge to meld together and form a single, very powerful entity. That magnificent deity was the sun god Atum-Ra, who brought light to the previously dark universe. His first feat of creation was to mold the primeval mound of earth—the ben-ben. (Thus, the priests of Hermopolis insisted that the sacred mound had stood on the site of their own city, not on Heliopolis.) In the words of the late Egyptologist George Hart, in the years following its appearance, the ben-ben became known as "the Isle of Flame because the sun-god [made it] and the cosmos witnessed the fiery glow of the first sunrise."[11]

The Power of Ptah's Words

Of ancient Egypt's four principal creation stories, the third derived from the country's first national capital, Memphis, situated roughly 30 miles (48 km) south of Heliopolis. As in the first two cosmogonies, the Memphite one featured the sun god Atum-Ra (later called simply Ra). However, the priests of Memphis were convinced that the prime creator was a different deity—Ptah. In Egypt's oldest times Ptah had emerged in that region as a protector of

An ancient statue of the god Ptah is shown here. Objects and living organisms were brought into existence by the power of Ptah's voice.

craftspeople, and over time he had gained prominence. Eventually, the locals came to believe that, although the nine members of the Ennead did play a role in the creation, Ptah had emerged long before them. At some point this earliest divine being decided to begin making other deities, and the first two of their number were his daughter, Naunet, and the future sun god, Atum-Ra.

The initial players in this story aside, the chief difference between the Memphite creation myth and the others involves the unique way Ptah went about making gods and other things. He did so by speaking them into existence. That is, when he named someone or something, that person or object suddenly appeared, fully formed. Such miraculous speech is mentioned in a surviving inscription carved on a stone at Memphis sometime in the eighth century BCE. It says in part, "There came into being from the heart and there came into being from the tongue . . . the form of Atum." In addition, "It is the tongue that repeats what the heart thinks. Thus all the gods were born [and creation] was completed through what the heart thought and the tongue commanded."[12]

This odd connection between the tongue and heart in the Memphite religious tradition shows clearly that the Egyptians, like most other ancient peoples, totally misunderstood the heart's functions. Thanks to the creation story involving Ptah and some other myths, they thought the heart, not the brain, was the seat of intelligence and personality. It was also believed that the gods could communicate with people through the heart. Meanwhile, people held that the function of the actual organ of intelligence, the brain, was to manufacture the mucus within the nose.

The Theban Cosmogony

In addition to the major creation tales emanating from Heliopolis, Hermopolis, and Memphis, a fourth one originated at Thebes.

Erected on the Nile's shore a few hundred miles south of Hermopolis, Thebes was Egypt's capital during what modern scholars call the New Kingdom (lasting from 1550 to 1069 BCE). Because Thebes was the nation's chief city during those years, its local priests were quite powerful and influential; and not surprisingly, they vigorously promoted their own version of the creation.

According to the Theban priests, the primary creator deity was a god with a dual personality—Amun. On the one hand, they contended, he functioned as a minor member of the Ogdoad. On the

In the New Kingdom, the capital of Egypt was Thebes (depicted here), the birthplace of the great god Amun.

other, in some mystical manner, he was also the mighty Amun-Ra, the strongest and greatest of all gods. In the Theban cosmogony, Amun somehow came into existence before the other members of the Ogdoad; moreover, he eventually absorbed them and went on to fashion the earth, the heavens, plants, and animals.

One thing that Amun did not create, however, was humanity. For reasons of his own, he entrusted that important job to another potent creator deity, the ram-headed Khnum. Long tasked with overseeing the Nile River's yearly floods and inventing pottery, Khnum was happy to help Amun with his creation duties. In fact, the two gods worked so well together and accomplished so much that the Egyptians came to call that dynamic duo the Lords of Destiny.

As for how Khnum went about fashioning people, a popular myth said that he used a special kind of clay—a silt found only along the shores of the Nile. Sitting at his large potter's wheel, he carefully molded one human body after another. Then he placed lungs, stomachs, hearts, and other organs inside the bodies and

Powers Inherent in Numbers

According to the Hermopolitan Cosmogony, the eight members of the Ogdoad fused together and thereby transformed into the great god Atum-Ra. It was thought that part of what made him great were various superhuman traits that derived from his divinity. However, also contributing to the breadth and potency of his magical abilities, the Egyptians believed, were certain deep-seated mystical powers relating to numbers. For example, the fact that the Ogdoad consisted of four pairs of gods was not random or accidental. Rather, in Egyptian society the number 4 was thought to possess certain inherent qualities that made it special in the natural order of things. One prime example consisted of the four cardinal points—north, south, east, and west—which people assumed had mystical importance. That is why the Egyptians made sure to align large buildings—like temples, palaces, and pyramid tombs—to face specific directions. The number 4 also affected the architecture of such structures. The three massive pyramids at Giza (near modern Cairo), for instance, have four sides each.

breathed into their mouths, thereby endowing them with a life force that allowed them to think and talk.

Khnum was also the key figure in one of Egypt's several minor creation myths, which claimed he had fashioned the gods and animals as well as humans. "Praise to you, Khnum!" states one of the inscriptions adorning his temple at Esna, about 55 miles (88 km) south of Thebes. "[Khnum is] he who the gods praise, and the goddesses acclaim, as the lord who fashioned them."[13]

The fact that the Egyptians accepted and cherished their many and differing creation myths suggests that they were fascinated by tales of beginnings. And in their devotion to their gods—the extreme piety that Herodotus noted about them—they were constantly thankful to the creator deities. Another writing at Esna, for instance, says, "He who . . . modeled everybody upon his potter's wheel" will forever "remain and appear in glory."[14]

CHAPTER THREE

Death, Resurrection, and Salvation

Far back in the dimly remembered past, not long after the great god Khnum created humans, another deity went out among the earliest residents of Egypt. His name was Osiris. One of the nine members of the sacred Ennead, he was at first a fertility god who ensured that the soil was rich enough to produce the crops necessary for people's survival. He also took on the important role of agricultural adviser and showed the first generations of farmers how to plant and harvest their crops.

Egypt's imagined first inhabitants were so thankful to Osiris that they asked him to guide them as their king. Flattered, he agreed to mount the throne as Egypt's pharaoh. As his chief adviser, and queen, he appointed another member of the Ennead—his wife (who was also his sister), the wise and kindly Isis. And for several years Egypt was prosperous and most of its people content under the couple's benevolent rule.

Of the few Egyptians who were not happy with the ongoing situation, the most influential was Osiris's and Isis's brother, Seth. Envious of his royal siblings, and power hungry as well, Seth plotted to slay Osiris and usurp the throne. Biding his time, he waited till Isis was away from the capital city and the king had scheduled a banquet at the palace.

That evening, Seth and his personal guards entered the throne room. Pretending that nothing was amiss, they carried with them a large, beautifully decorated treasure chest. After all the guests had arrived, in a friendly manner, Seth suggested that Osiris and others join in playing a special game. They would take turns lying inside the chest, and the player who fit the best within it would receive the expensive object as a gift.

One after the other, the guests took their turns lying in the chest. When it was Osiris's turn, most of the onlookers were surprised that he fit perfectly inside. However, Seth was not at all surprised. He had purposely designed the chest to fit his brother's physical measurements. And seconds after Osiris laid down inside, Seth's henchmen abruptly closed and locked the lid, trapping the pharaoh. Within a couple of hours, Osiris died from suffocation, and the henchmen threw the treasure chest into the Nile. Seth then seized the throne and declared himself king.

One unforgettable tale in Egyptian mythology refers to the fertility god Osiris (pictured) and his brother Seth. Power-hungry Seth sought to steal his brother's throne by tricking the god to lay in a beautiful chest.

When Isis returned to the capital the next day, she discovered that Seth had removed her from her position as queen and, even worse, had murdered her beloved husband. Though both horrified and grief stricken, she wasted no time in searching for Osiris's remains. Fortunately, she found the chest at the river's bottom. But she feared that Seth might find out and take the body from her, so for the time being, she hid it in some deserted marshes.

The Powers of Love and Magic

These dramatic events marked only the beginning of a much larger and momentous story. In fact, the ancient Egyptians viewed it as their most gripping and important myth. It became known as the "Myth of Kingship," in part because it defined the political, and more crucially the spiritual, dimensions of Egypt's highest political office. Yet the complex and compelling story did far more. It also dealt frankly with the concepts of death and rebirth, the survival of the soul, and the enormous powers of magic and love. The tale also taught the Egyptians about the world lying beyond death and explained how all people, not just rich and privileged ones, might attain salvation and eternal life.

The aspects of the myth that deal with magic and the power of true love come mostly from the series of events immediately following Isis's hiding of her husband's corpse. Regrettably for her, this move did not prevent the royal usurper from finding Osiris's body. While out hunting one morning, Seth and his henchmen stumbled onto the remains. Enraged that someone had rescued the corpse from the river, Seth sliced the body into numerous pieces. Next, he told his men to spread those bloody morsels from one end of Egypt to the other. Finally, Seth reasoned, he had managed to forever rid himself of his do-gooding brother.

The overconfident Seth was wrong, however. He had seriously underestimated the depth of his sister's love for her husband, as well as her amazing magical abilities. Driven by her love for Osiris, Isis searched relentlessly. According to the first-century-CE Greek writer Plutarch, she sailed "through the swamps in a boat of papyrus" and one by one found the scattered fragments of the body. Plutarch added that "the traditional result of Osiris's dismemberment is that there are many so-called tombs of Osiris in Egypt; for [to honor him] Isis held a funeral for each part when she had found it."[15]

Next, with the aid of her sister Nephthys, Isis carefully and lovingly pieced together the remnants of Osiris's body. The two deities then wrapped the restored corpse in clean linen strips, in the process mummifying him in hopes of giving him a decent burial. That act was destined to influence countless numbers of Egyptians in later generations because Osiris was "the first mummy," Egyptologist Bob Brier points out. "Almost every funerary belief

How People Envisioned Isis

The goddess Isis was by far the most popular female deity in the Egyptian religious pantheon. People associated her with a range of duties, qualities, and powers, among them magic, healing, and tolerance for others. She was seen as the nation's divine mother and the inspiration for love between wife and husband and between parents and children. A detailed description of her as people viewed her in the first millennium BCE appears in *The Golden Ass*, a surviving work by the Roman novelist Apuleius. When she walked among her worshippers, he wrote,

> her head was encircled by a garland interwoven with diverse blossoms. [At its center] was a flat disk resembling a mirror, or rather the orb of the moon, which emitted a glittering light. The crown was held in place by coils of rearing snakes [and] adorned above with waving ears of [grain]. She wore a multicolored dress woven from fine linen, one part of which shone radiantly white, a second glowed yellow with saffron blossom, and a third blazed rosy red.

Apuleius, *The Golden Ass*, trans. P.G. Walsh. New York: Oxford University Press, 1995, pp. 219–220.

that the Egyptians had can be traced from this story. For example, Isis [had to] recover the body and bury it on Egyptian soil. . . . [To the Egyptians] there [was] something special about Egypt and Egyptian soil. This belief is why the Egyptians never colonized, as no one wanted to die away from Egypt."[16]

Before burying her husband, Isis felt she should at least try to use her highly potent magical abilities to resurrect him. Sure enough, her application of several powerful spells caused the deceased pharaoh to steadily regain consciousness. Thrilled at being reunited, the couple conceived a child together, a male offspring destined to play a key role in their ongoing rivalry with Seth.

Following the death of her husband, Osiris (right), Isis (left) cast powerful spells to resurrect him from the dead. Once reunited, they conceived a male child that would play a significant role in the unending rivalry with Seth.

Reenacting the Harpooning of Seth

Because the "Myth of Kingship" was ancient Egypt's most important and popular religious tale, it is perhaps not surprising that it gave rise to large-scale and elaborate stage productions mounted by the government during major annual religious festivals. The biggest, most admired version was presented around 100 BCE at Edfu, 72 miles (116 km) south of Thebes. Several painted images depicting characters and scenes from the play have survived and can be viewed in London's British Museum. The late George Hart, once a popular lecturer at that institution, described those images, saying:

> In the drama, Seth is in the form of a hippopotamus and is shown in different scenes pierced by harpoons. The victors are the king [Osiris] and Horus, urged on by Isis. . . . The scenes involve ten harpoons, each piercing a different part of the hippopotamus's anatomy. Certainly a model hippopotamus would have been manufactured for the festival and have been the "villain" of the show. In the [images] the hippopotamus is shown diminutive [small] in stature, so that it could be contained and trapped [by Horus]. The symbol of the triumph of Horus is the depiction of him riding the back of the Seth-hippopotamus and spearing its head.

George Hart, *Egyptian Myths*. London: British Museum, 1990, p. 38.

Salvation for All Humans

Despite Osiris's remarkable resurrection from the dead, it seemed clear to him that, as a reanimated corpse, it was no longer suitable for him to mingle with the living. He told Isis that he must consult with the chief god, Ra, about the situation. Sure enough, Ra agreed that it was proper to assign Osiris different divine duties. And the two agreed that Osiris was now uniquely qualified to become ruler of the underworld.

Osiris's takeover of the realm of the dead marked a major turning point for the residents of Egypt. Before that, only the few rich and privileged people in the land were allowed to benefit from the gift of immortality in the afterlife. By contrast, when the poorer Egyptians passed away, their bodies decomposed and their souls slipped quietly away into oblivion.

With the ascendancy of the kind and caring Osiris as lord of the underworld, however, all that changed. Invigorated by his magical resurrection, Osiris brought potential eternal salvation for all humans. Even the poor could now enjoy existence in the afterlife if a panel of divine beings judged them worthy. Those who passed that test knew their souls were destined never to die and would enjoy the splendor of the afterlife. Osiris's netherworld kingdom was, in historian Rosalie David's words,

> a place of lush vegetation, a mirror image of the cultivated land of Egypt, that was situated somewhere below the western horizon or on a group of islands. This kingdom is sometimes called the "Field of Reeds," and the inhabitants were believed to enjoy eternal springtime, unfailing harvests, and no pain or suffering. The land was democratically divided into equal plots that rich and poor alike were expected to cultivate.[17]

The Instrument of Revenge

Although most Egyptians now loved and praised Osiris more than ever, one among them still despised him. His brother, who still sat on Egypt's throne, hated the fact that Osiris was back and more popular than Seth himself. Still, the corrupt pharaoh reasoned, at least neither Osiris nor Isis had tried to seek revenge for the deceit and murder. Hopefully, Seth told himself, he would enjoy his position of power over the Egyptian people for ages to come.

But this proved to be wishful thinking. To his dismay, Seth soon found that the instrument of revenge against him would take the form of the child that his siblings had begotten in the marshes years before. Now grown to manhood, Osiris's and Isis's son, Horus, decided that it was time for his nefarious uncle to pay for the crimes he had committed.

The intrepid young god launched his campaign against Seth by convening a meeting of several dozen gods. Horus requested their backing in his efforts to punish Seth and rule Egypt in his place.

Those divinities were divided on the right to rulership. They sat by in judgment while Seth and Horus fought over the throne. A series of encounters ensued as Seth and Horus attempted to outmatch each other and prove their right to rule.

Seth and Horus first clashed on the Nile's bank; Seth assumed the form of a monstrous, angry hippo, and to match this Horus did the same. The two plunged into the river and fought there for hours, each managing to draw blood from the other.

In a later battle, in which the combatants took their normal forms, Seth was able to distract the younger god long enough to get the drop on him. In one swift move, Seth injured Horus's eyes. Luckily for the badly wounded deity, the cow-headed goddess Hathor pulled him from the battlefield and in mere minutes miraculously restored his sight.

Horus duels with Seth, hoping to avenge his father and end the rivalry once and for all. Seth takes the form of a monstrous hippo (pictured) with the intent to destroy Horus and maintain control of his power.

As Horus rebounded and leaped back into the fray, another event seen by many as a miracle occurred. Both fighters suddenly halted, stunned by the appearance of a brightly glowing sphere in their midst. From that mystical orb stepped none other than Osiris. The lord of the dead began speaking, and his commanding voice echoed across the entire nation. Addressing Seth, Osiris warned that in the deepest, darkest crevices of the world below dwelled numerous terrifying monsters and other "savage-faced messengers who do not fear any god."[18] Those bloodthirsty creatures now took orders from Osiris. And he would unleash them on Seth if Horus continued to be denied the throne. Hearing this threat, Seth was overcome with naked fear, hastily gave up the throne, and departed the capital for parts unknown. In this way, Horus, having already been crowned king, finally took his rightful place as his father's heir. An Egyptian inscription dating from around 2000 BCE tells how Horus "was installed in the [former] position of his father, Osiris. He was told: 'You are a good king of Egypt. You are the good lord of every land unto all eternity.' Thereupon Isis let out a loud shriek [of joy] on behalf of her son Horus, saying, 'You are the good king! My heart is in joy.'"[19]

Hope and Reassurance for the Future

It turned out that Horus was the last god to rule Egypt. In time, he passed the kingship on to a line of human pharaohs. From him, these rulers retained a divine spark that made them part god in the eyes of the people. In fact, it was thought that each king became Horus while on the throne. Upon their death, the rulers then became one with Osiris, who protected the pharaohs' souls. The belief was that these connections with the gods ensured that the nation would always enjoy strong leadership and thereby endure.

Thanks to this single, highly comprehensive, and edifying myth, therefore, generation after generation of Egyptians felt hope and reassurance. First, their country would be long lived. Also, the tale assured the Egyptians that true love and magic were both real and powerful. Finally, and perhaps most crucially, all human souls could look forward to the potential of salvation and eternal life.

CHAPTER FOUR

Serpents, Soul Eaters, and Other Monsters

Each morning, Ra, blessed god of the sun and most exalted of Egypt's glorious deities, set out on his glowing barge, aiming as always to carry the bright sun across the sky. While the journey was repetitive, Ra hoped that each day he would face no obstacles along the path. Yet that fervent hope was always dashed. Inevitably, the evil and horrifying snake monster Apep (also called Apophis) attempted to overturn Ra's life-giving barge and slay the beneficent sun god.

Huge and hideous, Apep was a serpentlike being hundreds of feet long and weighing many tons. The texts of even the oldest of Egypt's religious writings were unsure of the creature's exact origins. One old story said that Ra's mother, Nit, spit into the primeval waters of Nun, inadvertently creating Apep. Another tale held that the monster grew from the corpse of a different evil creature that Ra had slain. Supposedly, that explained why Apep despised the sun god so much. There were other assorted myths about the beast's lineage as well.

Wherever the giant snake came from, its strategy was always the same. Each morning Apep hid below the horizon, just out of the sun god's line of sight. Then, as the glowing barge was passing over Bakhu Mountain, which helped hold up the eastern portion of the sky, the monster launched its first attack. For Ra to have done battle with Apep in the sky would have interrupted the sun's trek through the heavens, which the gods deemed unacceptable.

That is one reason why the sun god always carried protector deities with him in the barge.

The strongest of those protectors was Seth, a member of the sacred Ennead and brother to the great gods Osiris and Isis. As Apep neared the moving barge, Seth, armed with swords and other weapons, jumped out and confronted the beast. "Back, fiend, from the onslaught of [Ra's] light!" Seth told the monster (according to an early Egyptian inscription). "If you speak, your face will be overturned by the gods!" Then Seth reassured Ra, saying, "All is now well, O Ra! Proceed in peace! And you, Apep, Down! Away, Apep, O enemy of Ra!"[20] When words failed to stop the attack, Seth resorted to physical force. A battle ensued, and in some accounts, Seth sliced the great serpent to pieces. Unfortunately for Ra and Seth, however, it always sprang back to life in time for the next day's assault.

Therefore, Apep represented an ongoing, relentless threat to Ra and the sun's light and warmth; the monster was a menace to humankind and Egypt itself. It was no wonder that ordinary Egyptians feared and hated Apep and frequently performed ritu-

Apep, the evil and horrific snake monster, wanted to destroy the mighty sun god. Although Seth cut the monster to pieces, it always sprang back to life and became a representation of the persistent danger to Ra and his power.

als thought to both hurt the creature and help the sun god. For example, Egyptians commonly fashioned wax models of Apep and then spit on, smashed, and burned them, while repeatedly cursing the creature.

Beasts from Beyond Civilization

The ancient Egyptians were a highly creative, imaginative people, a fact amply reflected by the colorful characters and situations in their large collection of myths. Among the most imaginative of all were several hideous, scary monsters and other exotic creatures that were supernatural in nature but, for the most part, not gods. Most of the monsters possessed bodies having only animalistic traits, as opposed to the zoomorphic deities who featured some human qualities. In fact, often it was the lack of any redeeming human characteristics that made the creatures in question monsters.

To the ancient Egyptians, perhaps the most important aspect of the monsters in their lore was that people were absolutely convinced that such creatures were real. Moreover, it was thought that monsters dwelled in the remote, wilder sectors of the country, particularly in the sprawling desert regions lying to the west and east of the Nile. Just as a small percentage of people today are convinced of the reality of Bigfoot, the Loch Ness Monster, and the Jersey Devil, nearly all ancient Egyptians were sure that monsters lurked in diverse, dark, or isolated places ready to strike. As a result, periodic reports of sightings of such creatures in the wild were treated seriously.

Those sightings were most often made by hunters who roamed the isolated, little-known regions lying well beyond the bounds of civilization. That such settings were, in the public imagination, the main abode of dreadful monsters was not an accident. Rather, it spoke to the ancient Egyptians' general view of themselves. The common belief was that they were the most civilized, worthy humans in existence and that beyond the Nile valley lay mostly chaotic, treacherous regions that were sparsely populated by barbarous peoples. In the Egyptians' national consciousness, the desert was not merely a dry, forbidding area, it was also a symbol of the entire inhospitable and unfriendly world lying outside safe, nurturing Egypt. In historical writer Jimmy Dunn's words, hunting strange creatures and creepy monsters in the desert "became symbolic of subduing and taming the hostile forces that threatened the fertile Nile and thus Egyptian civilization. These fantastic animals became actors in this protective hunt for the benefit of Egypt."[21]

Doomed to Deal with Lethal Monsters

Among the creepiest and most frightening of Egypt's mythical monsters were those that guarded the afterlife. After Egyptians died, it was believed they had to be judged worthy of enjoying eternal life in the underworld. The lord of that subterranean domain, Osiris, and some of his monstrous assistants did the judging. Standing before them, each person's soul recited a long series of memorized statements, such as, "I have not blasphemed against a god" and "I have not robbed the poor."[22] These were supposed to prove that the person had not significantly sinned during life. If the judges accepted the truth of these statements, it was likely that the person would be granted entry into the afterlife.

If the judges deemed the person a liar and a sinner, however, that individual was doomed to endure the wrath of some of those scary judges, along with one or more of the most lethal monsters in existence. Tasked with punishing the wicked, these creatures bore names such as Blood Eater, Fiend from the Slaughterhouse, Bone Smasher, and Flame Grasper. Perhaps most terrifying of all was Ammit, who was nicknamed Devourer of the Dead, or Soul Eater. The very personification of divine retribution, Ammit had a crocodile's head, a lion's front legs, and the rear end of a hippopotamus. Individually, in real life each of those beasts is a powerful, fearsome killer, so the com-

Shown here is one of the most terrifying monsters in Egyptian mythology. Ammit, a creature with a crocodile's head, lion's legs, and hippopotamus's rump, was nicknamed Devourer of the Dead, or Soul Eater due to its gruesome conquests.

bination of all three quite naturally struck abject fear into the heart of an average person.

In such cases fear was a certain prelude to utter annihilation. In some myths, when Ammit ate a person's soul, that individual was immediately erased from existence. In contrast, a few contrary accounts claim that when Ammit devoured a sinner, the person's soul survived, but it was doomed to spend centuries, or even eternity, aimlessly roaming, or walking upside down, in darkness. In still another version, Ammit had misshapen, incredibly savage demon claws and mutilated the sinner's corpse with the soul still inside.

Taweret: Deity or Monster?

Physically speaking, like Ammit, the Bone Smasher, and other vicious monsters from the bowels of the underworld, most Egyptian monsters were largely hideous hybrids. True inhabitants of nightmares, their bodies and faces were usually weird nonhuman conglomerations of the most ghastly, repulsive features of animals such as lizards, scorpions, beetles, baboons, hippos, lions, and so forth. Yet although most of the mythical monsters had no human features, a few did. They tended to be zoomorphs that possessed particularly frightening or dangerous features or abilities.

A memorable example was one that seemed to blur the line between divine being and monster. Taweret, patron and guardian of pregnant women, with the body of a hippo, the legs of a lion, and the face of a crocodile, also bore some traits of human females, including very human-looking breasts. Modern experts think that these womanly attributes were what redeemed her from full monster status in the eyes of the Egyptians. On the one hand, Taweret was kind to and protective of women; on the other, considering that hippos, lions, and crocodiles were the most ferocious beasts in Egypt, she had a threatening side.

In one myth that displayed her beastly side, she became the demon mate of Apep and lent support to that serpent monster in its evil activities. Yet Taweret's forceful, monstrous side also played a positive role in Horus's righteous efforts to punish Seth for killing Osiris. As a historian at the Minneapolis Institute of Art puts it, "In the great myth of ancient Egyptian religion [i.e., the "Myth of Kingship"], Taweret showed what she was made of. Osiris, king of Egypt, had been slain and dismembered by his brother Seth. And when Osiris' son, Horus, rose to power, Seth sought to kill him too. But Taweret would have none of it. She held Seth down so Horus could take him out."[23]

Good and Bad Demons

That one of Taweret's myths pictured her as part demon is perhaps not surprising. Egyptologists have found mentions of more than four thousand demons in Egypt's surviving literary texts. A few of these creatures were, like Taweret, only part demon, while most were purely demonic. Many lived at the borders that separate the physical world and the divine realm, freely and ominously moving between the two.

The Princess and the Nasty Demon

The Egyptians believed that the category of evil demons included a few that sometimes inhabited human bodies. One of the most popular Egyptian myths tells how a princess almost died because of such possession. The tale begins with the renowned pharaoh Ramesses II falling in love with and marrying a beautiful princess from a neighboring land. One day, the young woman became extremely ill. The doctors who examined her told the king that she had been inhabited by a nasty demon and that they were unable to get rid of the creature. Hoping to keep his wife from dying, Ramesses hurried to the temple of the moon god, Khonsu, and sought his aid. Concerned, the deity agreed to help, went to the princess's bedside, and rapidly drove the demon out of her body. The demon feared Khonsu and proposed that a deal be struck. Namely, if the god allowed the creature to live, it would go far away and never bother any Egyptians again. Khonsu agreed to the deal, and the demon never returned to Egypt.

However, unlike the demons pictured by Christianity and other modern faiths, the full-fledged demons were not always murderous or otherwise dangerous or disreputable. In fact, Jimmy Dunn points out, in ancient Egyptian religion, "what we call demons were not necessarily evil." Many demons, he adds, "had protective qualities and, by their strange appearance, frightened many kinds of malevolent beings,"[24] including other demons. In that regard, Egyptologist Kasia Szpakowska explains, Egyptian demons "could be something like genies [in Arabian lore]. They would come to one's aid as often as they acted as fearsome, dangerous creatures."[25]

The Egyptians' belief that such mythical protective demons were real is demonstrated in paintings and carvings found in several surviving tombs. One is the tomb of a popular military general named Menekhibenekau. Carved relief sculptures decorating the main entrance show the deceased man's supposed journey to the afterlife. In one relief, the sculptor depicted six doors, or gates, leading into various sections of the underworld. Apparently, Menekhibenekau must pass through all six doors, and three guardian demons are posted at each door to make sure he makes it through safely. Among the names of these scary-looking guardians are He with Alert Heart, Eater of His Own Excrement, and Great One.

In contrast, plenty of Egyptian demons were downright evil or mean. Often, they spread disease, causing untold amounts of death and misery. In one common myth, Sekhmet, goddess of chaos, plagues, and war, had large numbers of demonic assistants who helped her distribute illnesses of various types. These demons, like many other kinds, were invisible to humans. As a result, they could be carried along by the winds, unnoticed by people, into almost any town, city, or region. In some versions of Sekhmet's myth, the demons were specialized archers

This golden statue of Sekhmet, goddess of plagues and chaos, was found in the famous tomb of King Tutankhamun, popularly known as "King Tut." In Egyptian myths, Sekhmet was often aided by various demons who did her bidding.

King of the Monsters?

The Egyptians were not the only ancient people whose myths featured griffins. Among the others were the Greeks and the early Iranians (who would later become the Persians). A hybrid monster like the soul eater Ammit, the Griffin, according to science and history writer Bob Strauss,

> features the head, wings, and talons of an eagle grafted onto a lion's body. Since both eagles and lions are hunters, it's clear that the Griffin served as a symbol of war, and it also did double (and triple) duty as the "king" of all mythological monsters and the staunch guardian of priceless treasures. On the premise that evolution applies every bit as much to mythical creatures as it does to those made of flesh and blood, the Griffin must be one of the best-adapted monsters in the Egyptian pantheon, still going strong in the public imagination after 5,000 years!

Bob Strauss, "Monsters and Mythical Creatures of Ancient Egypt," ThoughtCo, July 3, 2019. www.thoughtco.com.

who shot disease-ridden arrows out of their mouths. These explained to the ancients how illness spread through the land.

Giant serpents, soul swallowers, and a massive menagerie of demons made up only some of the strange creatures and scary monsters that the ancient Egyptians imagined lurking in their midst. There was also Babi, a baboon-like beast said to feast on human corpses; the Serpopard, a snake-leopard-cat hybrid; and the Griffin, a cross between a lion and an eagle. By today's standards, such creatures were beyond colorful and unusual. But as George Hart said, in fashioning their myths, Egyptian storytellers displayed the amazing "versatility of their imaginations," and in so doing, they left later generations "richer for their speculation and imagery."[26]

CHAPTER FIVE

Tales of Heroism and Adventure

In the mythic past, an Egyptian diplomat stood on the deck of a ship headed northward in the Red Sea, which borders Egypt to the east. The man was sad that his mission to make a trade deal with the king of Nubia, the African land lying south of Egypt, had failed. The diplomat was also quite fearful because he would soon have to tell Egypt's pharaoh about that failure.

At that moment, a well-dressed, clearly wealthy man approached the diplomat and asked what was bothering him. After the glum diplomat told his story of woe, the wealthy man urged him to cheer up. Negative situations often turn out to be more positive than expected, the wealthy one said, and to prove it, he told the diplomat his own story.

Years before, the now wealthy individual had been a poor young sailor working on a ship in the same waterway—the Red Sea. One day a terrible storm arose, and during the tempest, a towering wave struck the vessel and sent the young man hurtling into the water. A few hours later he awakened to find himself on a beach, surrounded by the wreckage of the ship and the dead bodies of all his shipmates.

By the day's end, the sailor had determined that he was on an uncharted island and that the only other inhabitant was a gigantic snake with the incredibly unusual ability to speak. The sailor at first assumed that the serpent would kill and eat him. But instead, the massive reptile took the man to its home in a nearby cave and made a meal for them both. The snake explained that it had been all by itself on the island for a great many years and was extremely lonely. So it was happy to have a companion.

When the sailor asked the snake how it had gotten marooned, the master of the cave answered that it had not been stranded there; rather, it had been born there in a colony of nearly one hundred large snakes. Everyone in the colony was content, the snake explained, because there was always plenty of food and the weather was perpetually pleasant. But then an unexpected disaster struck. A flaming falling star crashed on the island, destroying the colony and leaving the creature that was telling this story the lone survivor.

For the next four months, the sailor and the snake shared the island, and during that interval they became good friends. Then a ship anchored near the beach, and some people came ashore. Among them were some of the sailor's family members who had been searching for him. He urged his reptilian comrade to come aboard the rescue vessel. But the snake refused, saying that this had always been its home, and therefore it preferred to stay.

One heroic tale concerning the adventures of a shipwrecked sailor and a talking snake began with a terrible storm on the Red Sea (pictured).

As the sailor was about to depart, the snake said it had a goodbye gift for him. It turned out to be a treasure chest containing jewels worth a vast fortune. Enormously thankful, the sailor bade his friend farewell and returned to Egypt, where he enjoyed a fabulous life as one of the country's richest persons. Hearing the sailor's story greatly cheered up the diplomat. Perhaps, he thought, the pharaoh would not be awfully angry with him that he had returned empty handed. Thanking the wealthy man, he prepared to face the king without fear.

One reason that this tale, most often called "The Shipwrecked Sailor," was so popular in ancient Egypt is that it involves an adventure in a faraway land. Most Egyptians were poor farmers. Having never traveled beyond Egypt's borders, they were captivated by tales of sailors, traders, and soldiers who had visited distant places. In the words of the late Scottish folklorist Lewis Spence, Egyptians who did manage to visit faraway lands typically gathered "their friends and neighbors about them and [entertained] them with accounts of their travels."[27] Over time, the most popular of these yarns entered Egypt's always growing anthology of myths.

Why Sinuhe's Tale Remained So Popular

The ancient Egyptians loved the myth of Sinuhe partly for its descriptions of travel to a foreign country and the social customs in that place. But no less important to those who told and retold the story was its thoughtful commentary on life, nature's essential balance, and the workings of destiny. Here, the Egyptian belief in *maat*, a universal order or natural balance inherent in all things, came to the fore. Egyptians thought that when nature's order was out of balance, chaos, confusion, and injustice would follow. When Sinuhe fled from Egypt, where he was born and belonged, there appeared a disturbance in *maat*, which caused concern among the gods. Later, however, when Sinuhe went back to Egypt, the natural order was restored, and the gods were content. Thus, in ancient Egyptian eyes, fate and divine will guided Sinuhe throughout his journeys in the same way that these powerful forces helped guide all people.

An Extraordinary Traveler: Sinuhe

Without exception, the most famous and beloved traveler's tale in Egypt's long history was that of a daring and enterprising person named Sinuhe. The first known written version of his story dates to roughly 1800 BCE (nearly four thousand years ago). It was so often told and retold that modern experts label it one of the most important Egyptian myths; also, it is so well written that it is now seen as one of the finest examples of ancient Egyptian literature.

Sinuhe's story begins when he was a young man serving as a minor officer in the Egyptian army. Senusret, son of the reigning pharaoh, Amenemhat, is leading an invasion force in the deserts of Libya (bordering Egypt to the west). One night, while the soldiers are camped, Sinuhe walks around, checking on men wounded in a recent skirmish. As he is passing by Senusret's tent, Sinuhe inadvertently overhears the pharaoh's son speaking with a royal messenger. The latter reveals that Amenemhat had died a few days before, which means that Senusret is now pharaoh. For now, Senusret tells the messenger, this news must be kept secret.

Later that night, unable to fall asleep, Sinuhe is wracked by worry. What if the new king finds out that he heard what the messenger said? Surely, Senusret would punish Sinuhe for that. Finally, shortly before dawn, the young officer panics, deserts the camp, and flees back to Egypt.

When Sinuhe reaches Egypt, he feels that he has not fled far enough. Fearing that the new pharaoh might send soldiers to pursue him, he next journeys northward to faraway Retenu (now southern Israel). In that foreign land, quite by accident Sinuhe meets the local king, Ammunenshi, and the two become friends. Thanks to this unexpected and fortunate event, the Egyptian finds lucrative work, and over the course of several years he becomes

prosperous and happy. In a surviving ancient text of the myth, Sinuhe states that Ammunenshi "married me to his eldest daughter [and] made me chief of a tribe in the best part of his land [and] I passed many years, my children becoming strong men."[28]

Eventually, however, when he is nearing his sixtieth year, Sinuhe longs for his native land. He tells this to the kindly Ammunenshi, who says he understands and grants his son-in-law permission to return to Egypt. Once there, the self-exiled Sinuhe is surprised to discover that Senusret, who still sits on the throne, bears him no ill will. In fact, the pharaoh welcomes him and says that there had been no reason for him to flee years before. Senusret did not know that Sinuhe had overheard the messenger, and even if that had been the case, the king explains, Sinuhe would not have been punished.

Sinuhe is mightily relieved to hear that he is not in trouble and goes on to spend the rest of his life in Egypt's capital. Having taken a liking to his former officer, Senusret gifts him a clean, comfortable house with a flower-filled garden. "Meals were brought to me from the palace three times, four times a day," Sinuhe recalls when writing his memoirs. In the final chapter, he finishes the narrative on a positive note. "There is no [other] commoner for whom the like has been done. I was in the favor of the king until [my last day of life] came."[29]

From Architect to God of Medicine

Although these rather sedate stories of travelers like Sinuhe and the shipwrecked sailor engaged people's interest in foreign lands, mysterious creatures, and riches, the Egyptians also appreciated tales of heroes or scholars who were so accomplished that upon their death the nation's leading authorities deified them, or raised them up to semidivine rank or status. Some pharaohs, Spence wrote, working in concert with Egypt's high priests, called for the "deification of certain national heroes admired by the populace for their skill in learning and magic."[30] One such national hero was Imhotep, vizier (chief administrator), to the pharaoh Djoser (reigned 2667–2648 BCE). Imhotep had many talents, serving as the king's architect and the high priest of the sun god Ra. A learned man, he was a respected philosopher and writer.

This truly gifted individual was deified in stages, the first of which occurred in the first two centuries of the New Kingdom (ca. 1550–1077 BCE), around twelve centuries after his passing. By that time, a cult arose that venerated his name and his works. Though no one is certain what motivated his worship, the significance attributed to him as an architect might be at the heart.

An inscription on a large stone thought to date to the Ptolemaic Kingdom (332 BCE–31 BCE) credits Imhotep with the design of Egypt's first large pyramid-tomb, the Step Pyramid at Saqqara, in which the pharaoh Djoser was entombed. Before that, Egyptian royals and nobles were interred in one-story-high, flat-topped structures called mastabas. Imhotep's revolutionary idea was to stack six of them on top of one another, each somewhat smaller than the one below it. This feat initiated the main period of pyramid building in Egypt. The tale of this accomplishment—as narrated in the inscription—partly explains why Imhotep was so revered.

The Step Pyramid was the first large pyramid-tomb designed by Imhotep. Shown here is that structure, in which King Djoser was laid to rest.

The next two stages of Imhotep's deification took place in around 600 BCE and between about 400 and 340 BCE, roughly twenty-two centuries after his death. By 400 BCE he had gained a reputation not only as a deity of architecture but also as a great doctor and healer. He wrote influential works on injuries and identified disease as a natural process, not a divine punishment. He supposedly performed miraculous cures, and in one story, he entered a woman's dream and told her he would help her become pregnant. In still another mythical tale, Imhotep became one with Nefertem, son of the creator god Ptah. Eventually, his myth grew so large that Imhotep was equated with Thoth, the god of medicine. Much of this may also explain why his legend acquired a devoted following.

The Tale of the Clever General

Another real ancient Egyptian who attained legendary status was the military general Djehuty. He served as battlefield commander to the ambitious pharaoh Tuthmosis III (reigned 1479–1425 BCE). It was Djehuty's military genius that allowed Tuthmosis to defeat and seize control of what are now Israel, Lebanon, and Syria, turning Egypt into an empire.

The best-known myth about Djehuty's exploits depicts the semi-fictionalized version of how he captured the city of Joppa (now the Israeli town of Jaffa). The real events and his methods are unclear and still debated by historians. In the myth, however, Djehuty decided not to use battering rams on the gates or to scale the defensive walls using tall ladders. Instead, the crafty general turned to stealth and deception. First, he sent a messenger, who had been coached to tell a phony story, to the city's leader. The messenger falsely claimed that the Egyptian troops were starving and reluctant to fight. For those reasons, the messenger said, General Djehuty desired to give up the invasion, make peace, and go back to Egypt. Also, as a goodwill gesture, Djehuty promised to send two hundred unarmed men into the city. Each would

Was the Trojan Horse Based on Djehuty's Baskets?

In Greek mythology the hero Odysseus was said to have captured Troy (in modern Turkey) by offering a large wooden horse as a gift to the besieged city as the Greek armies supposedly gave up and sailed away. However, when the Trojans opened their gates and pulled the gigantic horse inside, Odysseus and his soldiers, who were hidden inside, emerged in the night to seize the city.

University of Oxford scholar Jorrit M. Kelder says that the Trojan Horse episode "is remarkably similar to the Egyptian story of the general Djehuty, who . . . captured the enemy city of Joppa by concealing his soldiers in large baskets." Some historians point out that the early mainland Greeks carried on long-distance trade with Egypt. Therefore, at least some Greeks were familiar with common Egyptian myths, perhaps including Djehuty's. The Greek tale of the Trojan War, including the wooden horse incident, developed a little at a time between about 1200 and 800 BCE. Homer, the Greek poet who depicted the conflict in his *Iliad*, did not mention the horse in that work. That part of the myth was added by other Greek poets, who may have based it on Djehuty's tale.

Jorrit M. Kelder, "From Thutmose III to Homer to Blackadder: Egypt, the Aegean, and the 'Barbarian Periphery' of the Late Bronze Age World System," Getty, 2022. www.getty.edu.

carry a big wicker basket containing all sorts of useful gifts for the city's inhabitants.

Joppa's ruler accepted these blatant lies and agreed to the deal. What he did not realize was that the clever Egyptian general had fooled him. According to a later Egyptian written version of the myth, Djehuty had each basket specially constructed to hold a heavily armed soldier. He told the men carrying the baskets, "As soon as you enter the town, you shall release your companions and seize hold of all persons who are in the town and put them in rope-bonds."[31]

According to the legend, the ingenious plan was successful. After the baskets were inside the gates, the men inside them sprang out and easily captured the surprised residents. Hearing the good news, Djehuty composed a letter to King Tuthmosis, saying that Joppa had been taken without the loss of a single Egyptian soldier. Djehuty became a national hero for executing this amazing plan.

The fact that fictional versions of the deeds of real people like Imhotep and Djehuty are still told and retold after thousands of years is no accident. It is a testament to the vibrancy, creative talent, and writing skills of a now vanished people. The ancient Egyptians are gone forever. But they left behind a fabulous treasury of timeless myths to their descendants—today's Egyptians—and to people everywhere who value good storytelling.

SOURCE NOTES

Introduction: Blueprints for Life

1. Toby Wilkinson, *The Rise and Fall of Ancient Egypt*. New York: Random House, 2010, pp. 15–16.
2. Herodotus, *The Histories*, trans. George Rawlinson. London: T. Fisher Unwin, 1886. www.gutenberg.org.
3. Quoted in Herodotus, *Histories*, trans. Aubrey de Sélincourt. New York: Penguin, 2003, p. 131.
4. Herodotus, *The Histories*, trans. George Rawlinson.

Chapter One: Maintaining the Natural Order

5. H.W.F. Saggs, *Babylonians*. Berkeley: University of California Press, 2000, p. 32.
6. Bob Brier, "Egyptomania: What Accounts for Our Intoxication with Things Egyptian?," *Archaeology*, January–February 2004, p. 18.
7. Joshua J. Mark, "Ancient Egyptian Mythology," World History Encyclopedia, January 17, 2013. www.worldhistory.org.

Chapter Two: Tales of the Creator Gods

8. Quoted in Josephine Mayer and Tom Prideaux, eds., *Never to Die: The Egyptians in Their Own Words*. New York: Viking, 1938, p. 25.
9. Quoted in Mayer and Prideaux, *Never to Die*, p. 25.
10. Quoted in Donald B. Redford, ed., *The Ancient Gods Speak: A Guide to Egyptian Religion*. New York: Oxford University Press, 2002, p. 251.
11. George Hart, *Egyptian Myths*. London: British Museum, 1990, p. 21.
12. Quoted in Byron E. Shafer, ed., *Religion in Ancient Egypt*. Ithaca, NY: Cornell University Press, 1991, p. 96.
13. Quoted in David Klotz, "The Temple of Esna: An Evolving Translation: Esna III," Bookdown, March 22, 2023. https://bookdown.org.
14. Quoted in Klotz, "The Temple of Esna."

Chapter Three: Death, Resurrection, and Salvation

15. Plutarch, *Isis and Osiris*, trans. Frank C. Babbitt, University of Chicago, September 7, 2020. https://penelope.uchicago.edu.

16. Bob Brier, "Isis and Osiris: Death and Rebirth in Ancient Egypt," Wondrium Daily, October 20, 2019. www.wondriumdaily.com.

17. Rosalie David, *Handbook to Life in Ancient Egypt*. New York: Oxford University Press, 2007, p. 142.

18. Quoted in William K. Simpson, ed., *The Literature of Ancient Egypt: An Anthology of Stories, Instructions, and Poetry*. New Haven, CT: Yale University Press, 2003, p. 125.

19. Quoted in Simpson, *The Literature of Ancient Egypt*, p. 125.

Chapter Four: Serpents, Soul Eaters, and Other Monsters

20. Quoted in Caroline Seawright, "Apep, Water Snake-Demon of Chaos, Enemy of Ra," Wayback Machine, April 4, 2004. https://web .archive.org.

21. Jimmy Dunn, "Beasts of Ancient Egypt," Tour Egypt. www.tour egypt.net.

22. Quoted in Miriam Lichtheim, ed., *Ancient Egyptian Literature: A Book of Readings*, vol. 2. Berkeley: University of California Press, 1975–1976, pp. 124–25.

23. Minneapolis Institute of Art, "Why Taweret Is the Ancient Egyptian Hippo Goddess We Need Now," January 11, 2019. new.artsmia .org.

24. Dunn, "Beasts of Ancient Egypt."

25. Quoted in Eric A. Powell, "The World of Egyptian Demons," *Archaeology*, May/June 2022. www.archaeology.org.

26. Hart, *Egyptian Myths*, p. 8.

Chapter Five: Tales of Heroism and Adventure

27. Lewis Spence, *Ancient Egyptian Myths and Legends*. New York: Dover, 1990, p. 190.

28. Quoted in Miriam Lichtheim, ed., *Ancient Egyptian Literature: A Book of Readings*, vol. 1. Berkeley: University of California Press, 1975, pp. 226–27.

29. Quoted Lichtheim, *Ancient Egyptian Literature*, vol. 1, p. 233.

30. Spence, *Ancient Egyptian Myths and Legends*, p. 303.

31. Quoted in Simpson, *The Literature of Ancient Egypt*, p. 83.

Books

Heather Alexander, *A Child's Introduction to Egyptology: The Mummies, Pyramids, Pharaohs, Gods, and Goddesses of Ancient Egypt*. New York: Black Dog and Leventhal, 2021.

Charles River Editors, *Heliopolis: The History and Legacy of Ancient Egypt's Cult Center for the Sun God Atum*. Ann Arbor, MI: Charles River Editors, 2019.

Virginia Loh-Hagan, *Horus*. North Mankato, MN: 45th Parallel, 2019.

Morgan E. Maloney, *Gods and Goddesses of Ancient Egypt: Egyptian Mythology for Kids*. Berkeley, CA: Rockridge, 2020.

Lucas Russo, *Uncovering Egyptian Mythology*. Independently published, 2022.

Philip Steele, *The Magnificent Book of Treasures: Ancient Egypt*. San Rafael, CA: Weldon Owen, 2021.

Billy Wellman, *Egyptian History and Mythology*. Independently published, 2022.

Internet Sources

All That's Interesting, "44 Ancient Egypt Facts That Separate Myth from Truth," July 22, 2020. https://allthatsinteresting.com.

Genevieve Carlton, "The Creepiest Myths and Legends from Ancient Egypt," Ranker, January 27, 2021. www.ranker.com.

Glencairn Museum, "Ancient Egyptian Creation Myths: From Watery Chaos to Cosmic Egg," July 13, 2021. www.glencairnmuseum.org.

K. Kris Hirst, "Osiris: Lord of the Underworld in Egyptian Mythology," ThoughtCo, September 4, 2019. www.thoughtco.com.

April McDivitt, "The Ennead of Heliopolis," Ancient Egypt: The Mythology, December 11, 2019. www.egyptianmyths.net.

Even Meehan, "Isis," Mythopedia, December 8, 2022. https://mythope dia.com.

Evan Meehan, "Ra," Mythopedia, November 29, 2022. https://mytho
pedia.com.

Rick Riordan, "Meet the Egyptian Gods," Rick Riordan personal website. http://rickriordan.com.

Websites

Ancient Egypt Site
www.ancient-egypt.org
Belgian Egyptologist Jacques Kinnaer writes and updates the text of
the many pages of this colorful presentation of ancient Egyptian history
and culture.

Ancient Egypt: The Mythology
www.egyptianmyths.net
This website provides detailed information about the gods, goddesses,
and religious beliefs of the ancient Egyptian people.

Mysteries of Egypt, Canadian Museum of History
www.historymuseum.ca/cmc/exhibitions/civil/egypt/egcr10e.html
This excellent site presents an overview of the main Egyptian gods, with
links to separate articles about those deities.

INDEX

PICTURE CREDITS

Cover: Klamann Hobbyphotograpy/Shutterstock

 6: The Stapleton Collection/Bridgeman Images
10: Vladimir Zadvinskii/Shutterstock.com
13: Qin Xie/Alamy Stock Photo
15: matrioshka/Shutterstock
20: Gado Images/Alamy Stock Photo
23: Imagedoc/Alamy Stock Photo
25: © NPL - DeA Picture Library/Bridgeman Images
29: Ivy Close Images/Alamy Stock Photo
32: Martina_L/Shutterstock
35: The Print Collector/Alamy Stock Photo
38: Lebrecht Music & Arts/Alamy Stock Photo
41: Duncan1890/iStock
44: Peregrinel/Alamy Stock Photo
47: Lostsurf/Shutterstock
50: World History Archive/Alamy Stock Photo
52: Bildarchiv Steffens/Bridgeman Images

ABOUT THE AUTHOR

Classical historian and award-winning author Don Nardo has written numerous acclaimed volumes about ancient civilizations and peoples. They include more than sixty overviews of the mythologies of those peoples, including the Sumerians, Babylonians, Egyptians, Greeks, Romans, Persians, Celts, Chinese, and others. Nardo, who also composes and arranges orchestral music, lives with his wife, Christine, in Massachusetts.